I0902116

Route 460

Red Rook Press

Paperback: 979-8-9929709-1-3
Ebook: 979-8-9929709-2-0

First paperback edition April 2025
Cover design: Anna Luis

Printed by Mixam in the United States of America.

Red Rook Press
Box 870244
The University of Alabama
Tuscaloosa, AL 35487-0244

redrookpress.org

ROUTE 460

P - - O - - E - - M - - S

savannah s. miller

Route 460

Route 460

For M & P

Route 460 takes its name from the highway running through southern Virginia. Pockmarked by speed traps and soybean fields, it was the road you took to get away. It was also the road you took to come back.

opening up

In my mind, I rewrite history, and
the West was never won.

The Puebloans still lay claim to the baked clay, and
the meteor veers off course.

With no need for Marx,
he sips tea in a communal café.

The Rio Grande never becomes
a border or political quarry.

Tiktaalik sinks to the ocean floor.
Pisano accounts for estuarine.

Pontius Pilate pardons Jesus and Barabbas both.
God forgives us on His own.

My father goes to therapy.
Gregory lets the cats live.

The serfs revolt.
The rats never arrive.

Babel never falls.
Lines never snag.

My mother tells me what she wants.
Judi gets out of that car.

The light in my cousin's eyes
never dims.

Princess Diana
never marries.

The humans
never die.

You are
never born.

Monsters Inc

When I was young, my mom had a jar
on the kitchen counter where she
dropped coins and small bills. We called
it "Mom's Secret Stash" even though it
was in plain view. She would go
weeks depositing the contents of her pockets
every night as she crossed the threshold, tired
of teaching and other forgotten jobs. Then a
day would come when I'd be struck
by an ad on the television or a friend's
rave review and beg to go see the next
big blockbuster. I would pester enough
until she agreed to take me, and we would
drive to the local grocery store. My mom
would dump her secret stash in the
coin counter, sorting pennies from dimes to
get her cash back. She would fold
the bills neatly and return them to
her pockets before taking me to the
theatre. She used that money to open
my eyes to the world around me, to
expand my concept of what was possible, and
it all came from this round jar on
the kitchen counter. I am older now and
things are better, but even so, I must
admit I sometimes miss those days, staring
up at silver screens with Joleen.

Trekking

I wish my dad had been Ben Sisko
On DS9, saving the world and making it home
In time for supper.

Jake could talk to him about everything and
Knew the kind of man he should be,
The type that tries

To be kind and understanding, supportive and
Steadfast, a captain and a cheerleader that people
Unite behind.

If Ben Sisko was my father, he would
Make me jambalaya and keep the changelings
Away, except for Odo

Because he knows better than to judge on
Appearances. He would want me to try and
Love me when I fail.

If Ben Sisko was my father, maybe then
I would know what I was doing instead of
Floating, lost in space.

Papa

My grandfather is
An honest man
Whose life may
Be broken down
Into three moments.

One: he finds
Himself alone on
Foreign sands watching
A missile climb
Upward, threatening him
And his future
An ocean away
But it is
Only a Russian
Satellite for science.

Two: The birth
Of his daughter
After mourning one
For five years
That signals he
Has not been
Abandoned by God,
A Thanksgiving miracle.

Three: His darling
Wife falls down
While inside a
Church back room
So he must

Sound the alarm
And call the
Kids who worry
But as he
Tells his daughter
To hurry along
Despite being a
Soldier he cannot
Help but cry.

There are other
Moments that belong
Solely to him
I cannot share.

unnamed

in the fourth grade my best friend was a weird girl
like me / she had red hair and two hearing aids from
a lack of oxygen / we made quite the pair / a chubby
queer girl who didn't know herself and a girl
just happy to be alive / i enjoyed her company
because even though she was blind i felt like
she saw me / she sat beside me at my birthday
party / we ate pizza and talked about how we wished
we could travel up mountains and not have to worry
about coming back down / two days later she was in
the hospital with a broken brain / she died and i cried
when i realized i never gave her a party favor / to this day
i wonder if she died not knowing i was grateful for her
presence

Game Day

When you think of me,
I like to imagine that
You remember us
Drinking state-issued
Chocolate milk
And eating pizza
For breakfast
Under fluorescent lights,
Talking about
Friday night plans,
Back before I fell
Off the edge
Of the ocean and
Away from you.

Upon Changing My Address

As a child, I used to dream only of leaving,
of adventures to different worlds using

foreign tongues that those who knew me
then had no desire to learn. I looked out

car windows at fields rolling by, spotted by
mom-and-pops waiting to be killed by time

and a pandemic, flashes of blue shutters
on houses where mothers drank wine and

children got lost to screens and both waited
for father to come home, always later than

he was meant to. I dreamed of
skyscrapers and a horizon line without a

single leaf or tobacco plant, somewhere the
weight on my shoulders was shared by a

million others within city limits, where
strange faces meant stories and adding to

my mythologies and never needing to
understand because I knew I never could,

and I also knew that was okay. Now I
am there, and I dream only of my

mother's face, my grandmother's chicken pie
on Sundays, my grandfather's Southern

drawl as he told me about his life, shelling
butterbeans at the kitchen table. I dream of

autopilot drives on dirt roads knowing when
to slow down for the cops at the corner, the

gas station stops that felt like social hours as
the ladies in church hats put twenty on five

and lipstick on their faces, the rearview mirror
as their guide. I dream of the responsibility

of breaking barriers and being the catalyst,
a big fish in a small pond making waves that

lap at my neighbors' feet, showing them that
they will remember me always. I dream of

being the town gossip because at least then
I know I am being remembered.

Yet, there is nothing for me there, and there
may be nothing for me here, and I wonder if

there is something for me anywhere.
Mornings I confront my mortality in a bowl of

graying milk, the true color of skyline, and
dream of dunking my head beneath it and

screaming. I numb my thoughts with yellow
bottles and book trips to San Juan, hoping

the beaches in my blood might help me feel
again in a way that does not hurt. I pull my

lover to me and thank God some strange faces
do not stay strange before the guilt of my

homesickness overtakes me and confusion
rattles my bones. One cannot be homesick

without a home, so I resign myself to nostalgia
for those amber days when I fell asleep on the

couch knowing I was safe and someone would
eventually come to pull a blanket up to my

chin. I wonder if I will ever feel
so cared for in my life again.

Mid-Lecture

Four cups of coffee in, I fight
sleep by cataloging the qualities
of humans in the room.

Handlebar mustache and tan
skin, a football player's shoulders.

Blonde hair and large nose, the
scarred knees of a skater.

Calico glasses and yellow
pants, the hair loss of a father.

Flag tattoo and sweater, the
black eye of a Nazi.

Senseless shirt and flip
phone, the heartache of a poet.

Bruised ego and undone
nails, the bagged face of a lover.

Red lip and brown teeth,
the energy of a python.

Gray strand and pink phone, a
chocolate orange sweetness.

Heavy lids and beauty
mark, desire prison bars.

Top bun and a nametag,
a working woman's calves.

Tiring of monotony,
these ghosts sing
me to   sleep

For Professor Orleck in May

I want to write a poem today, but I just can't seem to focus. My favorite professor was arrested today. A friend sent me a video of her sixty-five-year-old body being thrown on the ground by men in riot gear. She was just standing there. When I took her class eight years ago, I didn't know what I was doing but I knew what I felt, and that had been a good enough place to start. She showed me that Jane Fonda was more than a workout diet and let me read Emma Goldman. She threw her sixty-five-year-old body between the police and her students. She said that fast food workers deserved the right to live, and why was that such a novel concept to me then. Her sixty-five-year-old body lifted in the air. She has white hair like my grandmother. She heads Jewish Studies. She believes in freedom. Her sixty-five-year-old body landed on her bad shoulder. She told me about her partner and their kids. I wrote my first Chicago-style essay for her. I saw her sixty-five-year-old body hit the ground, and why did I keep watching. She always put her money where her mouth was. I learned how powerful I can be and how to make sure that means something. She said she was asking the police for her phone. Her sixty-five-year-old body was trying to make it home to her family. I came out exactly a year after my first class with her, and why had I been so scared before. People are cancelling their appearances on campus. Good for them. When I have a sixty-five-year-old body, for what cause will I lay it down. I envision a world without causes. She taught me that, and so did Emma Goldman. How am I supposed to write a poem when people are dying. How am I supposed to write a poem when the better generation is being arrested. How am I supposed to reach a sixty-five-year-old body. The ocean is rising. People are dying. You can't stay inside. The hospitals are overcrowding. People are dying. No one has enough money. Jeff Bezos has all the money. Twitter became X. You can't post the truth there anymore. People are dying. I know why I was scared. Her sixty-five-year-old body made a noise when it hit the ground. They were there because they were scared. People are dying, and where does it end. She was banned from campus.

Hangover

Friday night comes around and my friends
Drink their weight in bitter liquor until
They lose the traces of themselves
They claim are undesirable.
Brazen confidence overtakes their
Sweet and trusting dispositions and
The corners of their mouths twist
As they become conquerors and
Lovers and jesters and fighters.
I wish they knew how beautiful
They are when they're sober, how
Their eyes are bright with life and smiles
So genuine they become contagious.
I fell in love with my friends for who
They are on a Monday morning,
Groggy with sleep but optimistic
For the day ahead, the clarity of
Their vision letting them see that
Their futures are so beautiful.
They don't see that on a Friday night
When their judgement is clouded by
Strobe lights and vodka tonics and
They are looking for love in strangers
Who do not recognize the real them.
They mistake adrenaline for happiness,
An 808 drum for a heartbeat, and
In the morning they will wake up with
A clouded memory and pounding
Skull with fractures representing
The way they see themselves.
I wish they knew how happy I am

To know the real them, that I love
Their company in all its forms
Regardless of time of day or the
Alcohol in their blood, that the
Things which make them self-conscious
Endear me to them and make me
Feel blessed to witness how
They grow and change with each
Wrinkle on their faces. Yet, still
On those Friday nights my friends try
So hard to become the people they are not,
And while I miss them I am struck
By the fact that when my friends drink
I raise my glass with them.

gen z comedian

I'm so broke—
(How broke are you?)
I eat jokes for dinner.

I'm so broke—
(How broke are you?)
I line my purse with poetry.

I'm so broke—
(How broke are you?)
I have no time to write.

I'm so broke—
(How broke are you?)
I'm already bored.

Lessons

The morning sun crept through the bedroom window,
and I was jealous of the way it touched your face,
as I breathed in the scent of you I've come to know like
the smell of grandma's cooking on Sundays.

We've talked about why you're scared of comedies
and how everything must come in threes,
and even though neither of us has said that word yet,
I feel it blooming in the pit of my stomach

like a palm tree,
resting on a beach with the same sun on my shoulders.
I am learning to be at peace,
just like I am learning to let myself

fit into you when you pull me back in
for five more minutes.

Down

there is something inherently demonic about elevators
maybe that is why a young couple press together once inside
stealing kisses as the metal doors entomb them within
whispering words of adoration to each other when no one sees
she fills his cup and he fills her up with sweet nothings
that amount to little more than a false sense of security
and she will swear she is in love with the stranger in her arms
he feels beneath the fabric of her shirt as they descend
confident that he will win before they reach the bottom
and in blood she signs her soul away to a charmer
who sticks his tongue between her lips as if to consume
she has drifted into a dream where she is safe and loved
buying the lies that linger in the stale metallic air
smiling as uvulas crash and hungry breaths are traded
oblivious to the fact that when she awakens alone
she will be in hell and abandoned by lucifer himself

An Apology to Megan Thee Stallion

i'm so sorry megan but i don't think i can be your hot girl anymore see my therapist thinks i'm putting a lot of pressure on myself and my doctor says the same about my knees see i started taking longer to get up in the morning and it's hard to be a hot girl without summer see megan please don't be disappointed in me i really tried to be a baddie but i'm not from h-town and i really do feel like everything is my fault see megan i meant to be a savage but my body hurts from carrying the weight of generations so please forgive me megan see these wet ass tears keep flowing and no one seems to understand me and i know i'm pushing everyone away i'm just so sorry megan see it's just that sometimes it gets so hard to breathe that my air comes out as nothing more than a hiss

Cereal Dater

I left Cheerios for Froot Loops today
It just wasn't working out
After Lucky Charmed his way into my bed
And K proved to be anything but Special
I don't trust any man who says he's good for my heart
I'm so tired of being alone
Sad from Corn Pops with bad jokes
And Apple Jackasses who yell
And Frosted Flakes who never show up on time
It's days like this I remember
The man who hit me up just for Kix
And left thinking he knew me
Or the Cinnamon Crunch that got toasted
And forgot my birthday
Rice Krispy, who snapped, crackled,
And popped off on me
About his gender norms from the Golden Graham age
I've dealt with so many flavors of Wheaties
That ultimately all taste the same
I Krave a real love that's constant
One who knows my All Bran and loves it still
Even when I become soggy Grape Nuts
We'll split all the Chex at the restaurants
He'll call me his Honey Bunch and smile
And we'll be equal partners in this thing called Life

Maybe it'll work out this time
But if not
I'll just drown in a bowl of milk

Hunger

Lately I have been starving myself
Of the love I do not feel I deserve
Counting calories and broken promises of
I will always be there
And it is hard to remember
Any other taste but
Bitter.

When I was younger
Creamsicle ran down my lips
And you kissed it off me
Soft as the sun
On falling leaves but
Then the sun went away
And so did you.

I spent years purging myself of you
Trying to cleanse my body
Of the fingerprints
You left behind there
Wishing I could carve my ribs where
Your hands left marks
Trying to force them together.

My mother tells me
I look the best I have in years
Because now she can wrap
Herself around my body
With only one hand and
I have gained the weight of loss and
Lost the weight of myself.

In Tennessee

Late at night sometimes,
I pray to W.C. Handy and Elvis and B.B. King,
And I will them to bring you back to me.
I walk along the city streets of song,
Delta blues and sunny skies,
And I imagine that the reason it is not pouring now
Is because all the water has found refuge in me
And is causing me to drown inside out.
A heart broken in Tennessee
Does not recover like other hearts might,
For it is hard to heal in a place of music so beautiful
And so sad that it imbeds every building,
Finds solace in the cracks of the sidewalk,
The same ones we used to walk together.
I cried over a plate of fries from Huey's,
The one a block from your work,
And as I stared at the food on my plate,
I willed myself to remember how to eat.
I hear jazz music lofting through the Square,
And I wonder to myself if I might find you there,
Sitting amongst the people in love,
You the one who gave it up,
But I make myself pass by the open club doors.
My friends tell me to focus on myself,
But I am afraid I don't know how,
Having spent so much time trying to convince you
To just let yourself be happy
That now I have forgotten myself.

Rinse Cycle

I'm not saying that God forgot about me,
but I am saying that my clothes still smell like laundry water,
and I am a quarter short at the laundromat.

Division

A worm is severed in two by a careless child, and
thus begins a partial meiosis. Every good schoolgirl
knows a worm has as many as five hearts that must be destroyed
before the creature truly dies. Instead, each end becomes its own
entity, and the two halves of what once was go their
separate ways.

The new worm goes on
to become a strange soul in a familiar world, searching out
skeletons of the birds and broken mammals that will
allow her to grow new life in place of the old. She becomes
the businessman of worms, turning a profit
out of the dirt and death around her, raising
the capital of the forest, using the consciousness
it was never promised to edge
through sidewalk cracks like daisies, and though
she has conquered the new world, she is plagued by
the nagging sensation that it was not supposed to be this way
at all.

The old worm learns to move on: She seeks
refuge from rain waters on oiled pavements
lined by pedestrian walkways and trailheads. She eats
decomposing purple flowers to bring color back to her face and
burrows in the soil, a cocoon of manure protecting her from
morning vipers, and eventually, she creates a life on her own, fulfilled
by her place in the cycle, finding her worth in relation
to others. Still, as she navigates expertly through the world,
she feels a pit of loss in her stomach that comes when
a part of the self
goes missing.

One day the two worms meet and embrace,
but there is no recognition. Someone with no knowledge
of the world has used his ill-wielded knife to split the universe, shifting
the course of two worlds that were never to
exist in the first place.

Fragile

I fell in love with a boy made of broken glass
Bound together by chicken wire and
Bid to stay upright by those who call on Sundays.

I begged him to let me in but there was no in to find
Barely some pieces having cracked to expose
A cavern where his heart may have been.

I begged him to let me love him but
He doesn't know what the word means
Definition desecrated and defiled by pretty girls before me.

I fell in love with a boy made of broken glass
And even though I wasn't the one to break him
I still felt the shards when I held his hand.

As I felt my blood run down my fingertips
I tried not to notice but still
There is a—
                    Drip
                    Drip
                    Drip
—a pool of me at his feet.

Vanilla Latte

9:32 AM on Botetourt St.
    And my coffee tastes like you—
Robust and warm with a bitter end.

movement

Writing a ditty on an airplane staring at my neighbor's
911 Memorial tattoo. He got the window seat.

My feet are in the aisle and the stewardess moves
Around them like an angel.

They say it's about the journey, not the
Destination, but I want to be there.

I am tired of transit—headphones blocking out
The world. I feel guilty complaining.

These are first world problems, as they say, but I
Feel so suffocated on a jet bridge.

I find little inspiration here counting blowouts on the
Ink of fellow passengers, sleeping with my head at 90 degrees.

I will enjoy the trip, but at the price of
A day like this and an overpriced neck pillow.

Nevada

I was meant to be in the Southwest, to have
my skin brown against the red rocks as
I broil in the desert heat. I was meant
to be abrasive like a cactus that grows despite dehydration,

speckling Puebloan landscapes and dappling canyons.
I was meant to be Grand, an energy vortex
capable of moving humanity to tears.
I was meant to be a friend to the rattlesnakes
and coyotes and cracked valleys, screaming to empty skies that
fill with my terror.

I was meant to be awestricken and striking,
captivated and insurmountable,
to affect and create effect in turn,
to call upon the wild things and welcome them
with no concessions at all.

Departure

Spent the week in Vegas and came to the realization my ex looks like a serial killer.
My boyfriend is like an anatomically correct Ken doll.
Slot machines are boring now—neon coyotes that don't cry anymore.
Desert plants are a different kind of fauna—needles and fronds.
Friends break up here; lives are spent here.
The road is called Paradise, and traffic is bumper to bumper.
My taxi driver Hohm used to live in New Jersey.
I'll tip him the same amount I spent on my tattoo last night.
Most of the rich people here aren't very interesting at all.
At least Hohm takes the time to ask me questions.
My flight boards in 53 minutes, and all I have is questions.

Did my ex kill someone?
Does my boyfriend care I'm not Barbie?
Do the bags under gamblers' eyes go away?
Do cacti miss the rain?
Do people ever recover?
Do they get where they're going?
Does Hohm miss New Jersey?
Do I tip enough?
Does money like other people better?
Does Hohm know what his name sounds like?
Does home know I want it back?

another visit home

Every time it gets harder and harder to leave you, to clasp your frail body in an embrace and remember when it hoisted me to heaven like an airplane or caught me as I fell from the apple trees in your backyard. I give you deadlines, so you can count down the days until my return, hoping motivation of the future will keep you here in the present with me. Was I selfish to leave? This town hardly resembles what I once knew, and you are another version of yourself too, but still mine. I may have left, but I carry you with me everywhere—in the strands of white hair on my head or my longer right leg. I see your smile when I look in the mirror. Never go, but if you must, know you are the dandelion seed that attaches itself to my breast pocket as we walk through the old farm—overgrown, dirty, and so beautiful still.

Savannah S. Miller

Boston Stimulator

Mama woke up paralyzed Monday from the alien in her back. The doctors said it would help,
but Papa called me anyway. He wasn't able to pick her up anymore as he had several times
before, carrying her across thresholds and lifting her over rain puddles. When I arrived,
he sat in the chair with his chin in his hands and watched as I carried her rigid body to
the ambulance outside, the EMTs standing there with cigarette pack outlines in their
pockets. Papa couldn't help her then, and he couldn't help her six years ago when
he watched her hip break on the linoleum floor, or six decades ago when he
watched her legs run red three months too early. He was able to help her so
many times before, but there has been an inverse function between age and
ability, and I have watched as the people I love have grown frail and the
tables have turned: They need me now more than I need them. But I
want them, and that is why God is punishing me. I watch the hands
that hoisted me atop tractors and shelled butterbeans at the table
become wrinkled and shaky, fingernails purple from phantom
cold. Still, I am selfish and want them as long as I can have
them, and these observations are the punishment for my
greed. They know they will be with Jesus when they
pass. They have bought their gravestones, sitting
carved in the church cemetery next to Mama's
parents. I pass them when I visit for Easter. I
do not want them to die, but if they must, let
them die on a Sunday so they have less
distance to travel to Heaven. Through
them I have realized that end is not
instant. It is a trickle, like a drop
of water leaking from a faucet
until the bathtub overflows, a
slow decay, the wilting of
rose petals in a darkened
room. I call them on
Sundays, and they
always ask me
how I am.
How am
I suppo
sed to
tell t
hem
that
talk
ing
to t
hem
mak
es m
e a
ngr
y at
God
?

Record Low Mississippi River

running along delta banks
beneath the Frisco and Harahan
screaming at the passing cars
that try to kill her with
every screech of a brake
crushing against the levee with
all the power she can muster
even at her weakest a titan
angry that we would ever dare
to challenge her on her
70-millionth birthday
exhaust fumes for balloons
discards for presents
presenting her a cake of
gasoline and the things
we no longer find important
failing to remember that once
she sheltered Huck Finn from violence
fed the Choctaw and Sioux
split the country from itself and
inspired the movement of generations
now repaying her kindness
with a slow unnoticed death

trad wife does blank verse

I. *surrender*

A mother washes laundry dirtied by
Her children in the gravel drive. Some time
Ago she learned that you avoid the black
And red spots, focus on what can be fixed:
The stains of sweat and muddy fingernails,
Not blood from scrapes only time heals—splotches
That fade to pink but never truly go
Away. She will find pleasure in the blank
Slate a white shirt provides, the promise of
A new day, a second chance to do it
Right for them. Clothespins cling to lines strung up;
A flag of forfeit waves in unseen wind.

II. *a love poem*

I've always known I would die by drowning,
Being so absorbed by something that it
Becomes the air I breathe, consuming me
From inside out. I've avoided oceans
And dipped my toes into chlorine pools to
Prevent the unstoppable. I've gulped down
Greedy breaths to fill my troubled lungs up
And felt them expand with relief, but now
I know my caution was in vain because,
My dearest, I fear I will drown in you.

III. *june's elegy*

She decorates her house with fake flowers
Because they are the one thing her husband
Cannot kill—less fragile than her dreams were
And less needy than her love. These will hold
Their color unless bleached by the cold sun
That bears witness to her melancholy
And burns her cheeks, run rosy from her tears.
If these flowers were real perhaps those tears
Could be useful and grow something for once,
But no—they are useless except to bring
Some yellow to her eggshell kitchen, like
A bouquet atop a forgotten tomb.

2 weeks

I quit my job today,
and the earth continued to spin.
Birds still called to each other,
and men still fought with their wives.
Wives still cried in the bathroom,
and children still jumped from swing sets.
Doctors still set broken bones,
and woodpeckers still gave me a headache.
Ink still marred white paper,
and leaves still fell in shades.
My life alters completely,
and the world does not change.
I still ask the question:
What am I here for anyway?

passing cows on the interstate

The first time I questioned God came from Job,
who lost the things that make up a life to

a cosmic debate with the Devil. God took
his wife and children, the lowing

cattle, and then his fortune, all to prove that
Job would stay loyal. For decades

he languished alone, kept the faith and was
rewarded by a new life, a new wife said

to be more beautiful than the first. I wonder
if his judgement was clouded by solitude, so when

she showed up on his doorstep, he was simply
grateful to find another face. God gives and

He takes away, and for a just being, I don't
always understand. When I see your face I worry

whether I am in the before or after. Are you
the love of my life or a cheap replacement? I know

how you feel, and I am scared to lose you, wasting away
for years, chasing imitations that

can never compare to you. The Bible says
Job was happy but I want to ask him

how that heartbreak felt, to lose the world
and still manage to bend your knees and pray.

Runner's High

A mile in and I taste the blood in my mouth
A ferrous reminder of the journey to go

I force air into my lungs with each stride
The body doesn't work like it is supposed to

My heart in my shoulder and my hands in fists
Beat against inches of sweat and saliva

It is in the moment where I push myself past breaking
That I think that I am dying

I ran a race once—five kilometers in thirty minutes
Rewarded with a participation trophy and vomit at the finish

Everyone cheered with what air they had left
And when my friends hugged me close I felt so lonely

I run on my own now to talk to the trees
And when they don't listen I talk to myself

I am slower now than I once was
But I am faster than I was before

Sometimes I pass women with their dogs
And sometimes other runners pass me

I wonder what they are running away from
Going so fast to nowhere at all except

Arbitrary markers like leaning trees and
Cars parked on the side of the road

There is an end in sight now past the park
Where they found that little boy last spring

His mother had been on the news and now I think
I hear her cries on the wind

Begging to go home
I cross the two-mile line

Doubled over I catch sight of myself
A reflection of a puddle from last night's rain

She is tomato red and sags with exertion and though
She hates herself she must admit she's beautiful

Her heart still beats in her chest and her mind
Cries victory inside its hardened cage

She's proof that what you can't see
Can still hold so much power

I heave in breaths of oxygen
I finally get it now

conception

you decide to stay and in that moment –
a phantom embryonic sac ruptures and you are reborn
a crocodile in the swamp –
          the mud embraces you

as its own you are blessed by the rain that
seeps through the cracks in your scales –
your eyes loom over the edge of the water
          you watch the fauna slowly grow through you

you become one with the algae
a piece of landscape –
          the rest of nature grows around
you have always been here an imprint in the fabric of time –
your teeth have left bite marks on wooden logs
          supporting the trial of atlas you have
          the power to upturn stones you have
          settled millennia on the bog floor you have
outlasted bodies made of peat – those that smile at you
lower than layers of bedrock
you have made friends with the entire world –

and you have experienced all of this
          felt this whole because
          you placed a foot on the ground

The Albatross

She takes to the sky and doesn't want to come down, sailing over
oceans for years and filling her body with krill that meet her

at the surface. After some time, when she is ready, she sacrifices
her face to the gods of the ground and dances for the world, who
looks upon her with bright eyes of adoration. They are in love

for life. She guides sailors out of storms and icy trails, beating her
arms to make the wind for them when they meet none. And then

she is shot down by the very men she is helping, her carcass
fashioned into a grisly necklace around the body of a killer. The
world mourns for her. The earth cries and wails for a lost ray, and

then it is silent. The sun rises and sets on new days without a
purpose,
and her spirit lets nature set the order right. Death comes for
those who

came for her love, and others commit her memory to poetry,
weaving
new myths from her paradoxical body that defies laws of physics
for she transcends what is knowable. Baudelaire

calls her *veule,* spineless, but for a Romantic, he should have seen
the
beauty in a being so unsure of her feet that she learns to use her
wings.

How you take it

She asks for
        2 cream, 2 sugar

because she wants / life sweet

He asks for
        2 cream, 2 sugar

because he wants / it black

But he knows
        2 cream, 2 sugar

isn't enough / for her

See, she wants
        4 cream, 4 sugar

but is afraid / to ask

And he wants
        2 soothe, 2 sweeten

so he will ask / for her

And I think this is love.

the ballad of billy fingers

wax poetic in
wayne manor bouncing
bubblegum boy patched
glass leaving stains
on his beard
tip tap atop
nikon camera dials
smile for them
please pretty teeth
perfect boy beautiful
boy john foresaw
his breath in
her neck he
burns stars on
his fingers espresso
jolt jump turns
dials exposure to
the elements wears
down a work
of art until
each stroke is
bared to gnashed
veneers but he
smiles for her
shaven eyebrows he
tells her about
the gridiron blocks
of the city
she cements him
in the ar-
chitectures
of pages she
hears funeral tolls
as she tip
taps into the
reddened soil along
the mississippi river
alfred consoles master
wayne and the

bats cyclone an
embrace wings wander
round and round
his dials turn
he spirals down
thought staircases leading
to a dual
past two homes
two mothers one
father and the
frauds he carries
with him diving
into tales where
goodness always wins
in colors of
contrasting reds and
villains are identified
by the puns
they speak he
finds the light
within her beating
jugular rocking robin
is nothing but
a dick and
in the end
bruce would have
been more beautiful
if he looked
like him before
the tennessee sunrise

Led Zeppelin

My mother always told me
True love meant ups and downs
Standing with each other in hell
But with you I have found
Something more like Heaven
And moments on the Stairway
When even in the darkness
I know just to hold your hand
And put one foot in front of the other
It is a faded band T-shirt
And my head in your lap
One too many pinot noirs
An old action movie on the screen
It is your hand in my hair
Firm enough I know it's there
Soft enough it doesn't burn
Like other hands did before
A step-by-step climb that leads
Straight to the clouds and
A pleasant ache in my muscles
And walks on Sundays
Through public parks
My eyes on the flowers
And your eyes on me

After Amsterdam

Inspired by Gregory Alan Isakov

He holds an unread novel in his delicate hand,
A photographer's fingers that are always
Turning dials in search of the light,
And his other hand is in mine.

We listen to Isakov in the air,
Split between two buds blooming
Miles above the Atlantic,
Living six hours in the future.

He has come dangerously close to my heart
And the scarred used tissues
Lost in a gambler's bet with God,
My lessons learned.

Rain on the window of the jet plane
Casting moonlit shards of dial light
Onto the scene of a movie
I swore I would never watch again.

Three names and three words,
Six strings and seven lovers,
And a song I can only strum in a minor chord,
Hoping the rain helps clear the head.

I have become used to being terrified
Of the dark and the monsters that lurk there,
But there are still stars
In the South above his eyes.

If he casts me away in throes of a dance,
At least I will have been a rag
That turned the dials for a moment in time
On his film forever.

Detour in Quincy, IL

bound by brown hotel bedding
next door to the hobby lobby
we do not go there
the speed limit is low and
slow seems to be the way here
the sun crawls across the
sky in frames of orange speckling
rows of long-haired corn
they will sell it too cheap and
switch to grain next year
this is the type of town
people pass through yet
homes dot the landscape and
give shape to the hills, curves
then jags like scars on
skin the people here move
slowly like the cars on
thirty-second street, the world
is quiet on the iowa border
across the water a different
world shades of yellow and
fetuses on billboards it is
an election year
names slashed against the sky
with slogans for change or
the opposite which does not
mean the same to them
shelter finds me in the
solitude of an air conditioned
room and the sheets turn
olive in the sherbet light

Takeoff in Charlotte

The Universe made the stars but we have made the constellations
Visible out a foot-wide window from 30,000 feet
Blinking gold and blue darts crossing avenues down below
Going somewhere always

I would find you at the end of Orion's outstretched arrow
Somewhere between the black patches of forest and speckled glow of suburbs
Your hatred burns the map lines red
Enshrouded face carved itself into the geography
Fingernails became skyscrapers reaching to grab me and make me pay
For what I did to you I cannot say sorry

I find myself miles above where you make your bed
The one I used to lie in as we counted stars through your curtains
Like a glove one size too small the circulation cuts off slowly
You never saw it until my hand fell away and the rest of me ran too

My sky is different now with Sirius guarding above my pillowcase
Jupiter and Venus consoling from the east
This was preordained by the stars
I was always meant to depart from you searching for something
Bigger than a fractured southern sky

Still my mind wanders to you with a pang in the pressurized air
I hope you are well without me and draw Ursa Major in the clouds
May you forget me and let my name become mythology
The woman who never was and who you never knew in exchange
I will connect through Atlanta and leave you to the Carolina fires

Homecoming

He let his coffee get cold on my
kitchen table; I suppose that means
he's settled in. I ponder over
lukewarm grays what made this any
different. He held my hand when
others dropped it and chased when
others turned away. He drips honey in
my teacup and offers to put the kettle
back on.

Anniversary

I have known your smile two years now,
But I swear I knew it before
When I was a child climbing oak trees
For a better look at the sky.

I have craved a love that once
Labeled me hopeless,
Something that drew stars in
The margins of notebooks,

Filled the pages of pink
Journals locked away from the world,
The only key dangling
From a chain around my neck.

They told me you did not exist,
And I languished alone,
Shaving my legs to act as a beacon
To ghosts of storybook characters.

It is difficult to fall in love with someone
You are not sure is real,
Like Bigfoot believers chasing
Footprints in Carolina mud,

But like a stranded follower
I kept the faith and moved
Through mountains and inlets
Step by step towards you.

If we melted all the books I read,
Salvaged all the ink from my poems,
Drained the rose gold from my eyes
To find some kind of meaning,

I think they would add up to you
Smiling in my passenger seat,
Placing a worn blue baseball cap
Atop my lifted head.

In Delphi

The tour guide talks of miles and voyages across the sea to wait for
some relief from the unknown of life.
An oracle—
High off bay leaves and desperation
Who listens to the tears of mothers and apathy of emissaries—
Sat behind the ruins under my feet.
I wonder if she predicted her own demise.

It seems ironic to build a place of such despair in a heaven like this,
To cling to the future when the present is so beautiful.
The children smile.
The sun gleams.
Apollo plays the lyre.

My thoughts turn to you as they always do. Would I have
come here for the knowledge of you,
Waited in line for a glimpse of your eyes and the hope that
everything would be okay in the end?

The wind across the Aegean slaps my face in reprimand—
Of course not.
Why spoil a gift from the gods?

The sun sets: Apollo chasing Daphne over the mountains.

In County Clare

To get to the Cliffs from Galway,
you must take a path called the Wild
Atlantic Way. As the name suggests,
narrow lanes weave up and down, left
and right along lush hillsides, past broken
castles, abandoned abbeys with
gravestones clouded with age and fauna—
life growing over the dead. Penny walls
reach skyward over centuries, reminders
of the brutality of humanity, a genocide
orchestrated by petty brethren
jealous of the gorse. People have forged
lives here in the rain and the wind
that, no matter how strong, cannot blow
the damn rocks away, knock the walls down,
and when you finally reach your lookout
point, awash with green and crashing
waves, you may find yourself
grateful to exist in the same time period
as chlorophyll and limestone, carved
by acid precipitation long before you were
a thought in the mind of the Universe.

On Mother's Day

You gestate inside me, the size of a kumquat. My darling,
you are painful. I lock myself in sonar worlds where I can
pretend you don't exist. This is all to distract me from
the knowledge that you are due any moment now, plotting
how to tear me open with your forming fingernails, ripping
nick to navel as you destroy me for sport. My blood pours
from my carcass onto white pages now unclean with
evidence of my sin. They will ask me what to call you, and
I will gift you a name made of nonsense and overstrung
metaphors. I carry on too long until you burst from me
your own person, as if you never belonged to me at all, and
I will stare at your face and wonder for whom or what
you were made.

Ars Poetica

After "The Poet" by Michael Kleber-Diggs

I.

She sits in darkness.

A hurricane has knocked down power lines by the
Village Inn, so now she sits in the shadows of her porch
and watches the rain. She is fascinated by cycles, how
nature pours its power out only to suck it back up again.

No one seems to understand her obsession with circles, how hearts break
and rebuild themselves, how daughters become their mothers. Still,
her eyes watch the rain, knowing she will only have this storm for a moment.

II.

Sometimes I get sick on a page—red wine
and nachos everywhere,
vomit bleeding into words. I have
a thought—if my intestines are
noteworthy, something to understand, or
nothing more than the gross insides of
a stubborn, selfish cryptid? But anyway—
how does it taste?

Acknowledgements

A large thank you to those who helped *Route 460* along in its creation—my friends and beta readers, Emily and KC; my mentors, Michael Kleber-Diggs and Lindsay Starck through the Augsburg University MFA program; and my loving family members, especially my mother.

Publication History

"Rinse Cycle" was first published with Ambidextrous Bloodhound Press.

"In Tennessee" was first published as "In Tennessee, Pt. II" with The Dead Mule School of Southern Literature.

"Fragile" was first published by Sad Girls Club.

"Hunger" was first published by Silent Spark Press.

"Vanilla Latte" was first published with Ambidextrous Bloodhound Press.

"Cereal Dater" was first published in Millennial Pulp Literary Magazine.

"unnamed" was first published in Gabby & Min's Literary Review.

"Runner's High" was first published by Rising Phoenix Press.

"In Delphi" was first published in Audience Askew Literary Journal.

"Led Zeppelin" was first published on the author's social media.

"In County Clare" was first published with Watershed Review.

"Down" was first published with Modern Language Studies.

"Record Low Mississippi River" was first published with Modern Language Studies.

The poems "Game Day," "Upon Changing My Address," "Departure," "After Amsterdam," "Ars Poetica," "passing cows on the interstate," "movement," "Nevada," "Detour in Quincy, IL," and "Takeoff in Charlotte" were first included in the chapbook *Transit*, published with Bottlecap Press.

About the Author

Photo: Brandon Dill

Savannah S. Miller (she/her) is a queer and disabled writer, theatre artist, and converted Memphian. She was the inaugural Young Playwright in Process through Young Playwrights' Theater in Washington, D.C., as well as a two-time winner of the Eleanor Frost Playwriting Contest. Her fiction and poetry have been published or are forthcoming with *Modern Language Studies, Jelly Bucket, Flash Fiction Magazine, Watershed Review*, and others. AB in Theater: Dartmouth College (2021); MFA in Creative Writing: Augsburg University (2025). Read more at savannahsmiller.com.

Red Rook Staff

Acquisitions

Olivia LaRose (liaison), Hannah Bazinaw, Lexi Burroughs, Aubrey Case, Caroline Cunningham, Soleil Demars, Charlotte Diel, Jordan Earnest, Malik Erskine, Camryn Haag, Kaira Harper, Angie Henle, Anna Luis, Kalyn King, Addison Lusco, Ainslee Monroe, Ava Rudd, Elle Sims, Scarlet Sodergren, Kiley Stevens, Alyssa Walker, Tatum Walker, Alyssa Wallner

Audio

McKenzie Knight (liaison), Elanor Asuncion-Crabb, Soleil Demars, Andrea Gonzalez Larregoity, Izzy Novak, Tatum Walker

Design Team

DeAndra Gauntt (liaison), Anna Luis (liaison), Anna Cobb, MiKayla Davis, Alexandria Gauntt, Elizabeth Golembiewski, Ainsley Greer, Andrew Kelley, Anna White

Poetry Editing

Jane Champ-O'Connell (liaison), Victoria Bell, Wrenley Brown, Caroline Cunningham, Malik Erskine, Aaron Hightower, Ainslee Monroe, Anne Stewart Rogers, Aidan Strebel

Promotions

Maya Mungo (liaison), Jackson Davidson, Camryn Haag, Kaira Harper, Sarah Vance Harrison, Kalyn King, Dante Larkins, Ella Lybarger, Hannah Mauck, Lex Mroczko, Averi O'Brien, Karmen Paige

Website

Ansel Smith (liaison), Henry Bowles,
Swastee Regmi, Luke Theobald

Mocktail Team

Aaron Hightower, Olivia LaRose

Special Projects

Wrenley Brown, Livi King, Karmen Paige

Faculty Advisers

Paul Albano, Sarah Cheshire, Merrill Lee Girardeau,
Stephanie Marker, Jane Morton

About the Press

Red Rook Press is an award-winning, student-run publishing house from the University of Alabama. Our goal is to foster and promote the creative minds of undergraduate and graduate students still establishing themselves in the writing world by giving them the opportunity to bring their voice to life. With our staff of dedicated undergraduates student-editors and professional advisors, we bring several new books of prose and poetry into the world every academic year.

Find us at redrookpress.org

Praise for *Rolling Windows*

Rolling Windows is a succulent, sultry refraction of digital sonics. Campanioni's poetics do not rupture the fourth wall inasmuch as they bring the poem and reader so close to one another that the veil of longing and exile constellates into a velvet of intimate inquiry. The poet spirals across media and data systems and returns from the outernets of bandwidth to ask, "what's the difference between a human brain & a hard drive / a hard drive & a tomb." This is a collection of playful, dexterous care excavating what the datafibers have numbed within the synapses, for "what's left behind when the body moves, when it collapses inward or elides touch." *Rolling Windows* peels away the coldness of what we have inherited from the computer age of colonialism and late-stage capitalism to rewire the body's sensory-memory. Campanioni is a poet of widening and wilding imagination who wades into digital fracture to glitch language toward staggering clarity.
—Anthony Cody

Chris Campanioni's *Rolling Windows* moves with the intimate urgency of Hervé Guibert and the theoretical precision of John Berger, but with an entirely contemporary slipperiness that belongs to no one but Campanioni himself. Here is a writer who understands that every text is a book of spells, that language passed "mouth to mouth" can transubstantiate reality into something better, stranger, more alive. These pages flicker between presence and absence, between the personal and the political, with the kind of revolutionary ear that Fred Moten would recognize—except this revolution happens quietly in the spaces between looking and being looked at, between message and presence. This is essential reading for anyone who believes that how we see determines how we live. *—Marwa Helal*

In Chris Campanioni's stunning *Rolling Windows*, an "erotics of indeterminacy" activates formal challenges to the digital nowness of screentime and its obscene elisions of human feeling. This is information flow as noetic ice floe, where the blur becomes the message: the end(s) of the earth seen from an archipelago of VHS tape detritus floating and whirring in the disintegrative climates of disaster. Metaleptic brain tissue is hardwired into a syntax of digital nomenclature, while deictic surges abound in the ether of intercourse and dromomania. The auratic capital of tactility necromances the fossilized remains of flatland romance in the swipes of desire and the wipes of contagion. Here, the mouth is still a vessel of lyric force, while the screen assembles a window-seat view into anthropocentric afterlives. In and against the encroaching waste land of trademarked A.I. Slop, *Rolling Windows* invites us to return to analog forms of desire: don't just wipe the screen or swipe the phantom, roll down your window, look out and feel the zephyr on your face, breathe in the battery-flesh of the world. *—Jose-Luis Moctezuma*

Praise for *Windows 85*

A work whose chaotic feminine essence transcends material. ... Campanioni toys with stuff you're not supposed to touch, and normies are right to clutch pearls. Postmodernism thrives on taboo. ... Compression and extraction, encryption and decryption —the yoking recalls a neural net's black-box insides. And yet the work portends rebellion against LLMs' soullessly sterile mien, Campanioni's a war cry for artists to meet ChatGPT in its nightmares. —Nat Alonso, *RHINO Poetry*

Agile, precise, flamboyant, and even promiscuous, equal parts postcolonial and neobaroque in exultant devotion to a literature of cosmology: Campanioni's exuberant style somehow defies the consumerist logics of late capitalism. ... Like shiny wrecks, Campanioni's poems denaturalize the technocratic norms of postmodernity and, paradoxically, refamiliarize readers with the singularity of their own sensations and perceptions.

—Kendra Sullivan, *Los Angeles Review of Books*

Poems full of slippages navigating various multiplicities, with the lightness and promiscuity of their language bouncing off the page ... more like encountering an avant pop album than a book of poetry. But of course there's a political undercurrent to all of this ... a fiercely contemporary thesis dismantling the perceived primacy of borders and binaries.

—Christodoulos Makris, *Books Ireland*

You're doing what the Cubists did to painting but in lyric form. ...

—Tiffany Troy, *Los Angeles Review*